Growing Up

Trevor A.

MW01064969

Introduction

Do today's teenagers and young adults face new challenges compared to young people from previous decades? Yes and no. Today's challenges are not new in the sense that people have never faced those kinds of temptations before. Satan's methods and the basic kinds of temptations have not changed. These temptations have been "common to man" (1 Corinthians 10:12-13) across the ages. However, technology that affects how frequently, quickly, and intensely Satan can tempt people has changed, and much of American society promotes a worldview that pressures people to approve of and give in to those temptations.

Some of these lessons about specific temptations may be uncomfortable to teach or discuss; trying to put a life back together that has been damaged by yielding to those temptations can be far more uncomfortable. While addressing difficult issues, keeping the focus of the study upon the relevant passages provides the best way to address these temptations with openness and propriety in the classroom setting.

I would be glad to have been wrong about how widespread these problems will be in our society over the next decade. Unfortunately, the trends are not favorable. Teachers should be watchmen who warn others of the problems and work to prevent or fix them (Ezekiel 3:17; 33:7).

May God help us to be "wise as serpents and harmless as doves" (Matthew 10:16) when it comes to handling these temptations. My prayer is that this workbook will help young (and not-so-young) people stand for truth in a hostile world.

Trevor Brailey, December 27, 2019

Table of Contents

Lesson 1
Ways of Thinking That Shape Our Society

The way you see the world is affected by the culture around you. Our culture almost certainly affects us in more ways than we realize. Can you imagine living in any kind of government other than a democracy? I have a hard time doing so. However, the majority of people and Christians throughout history have done so. It is helpful to remember when reading Paul's words in Romans 13 and Peter's in 1 Peter 2:13-17 that they were dealing with governments which they had no role in choosing and which would eventually oppose them to the point of executing them.

We should also learn that we cannot count on culture to guide us to please God – quite the opposite. We should not expect true Biblical teaching to be popular.

· What does **Matthew 7:13-14** show us about how much of the population in any society will be faithfully following God?

While societies will vary in how much they respect moral principles over time, we should never expect that any society will make it easy to follow God's word fully. The trend in our own society (The United States of America in the early twenty-first century) is clearly to move away from principles of Biblical morality.

· What are some examples you have seen of laws or rules that have been made (by the government or by the schools) that do not respect Bible teaching? What are some examples of practices or beliefs that have become more popular which oppose the Bible? (After this class, why not ask a parent or other adult?)

One of the key philosophies that affects people in our society in many ways is **postmodernism**. After numerous scientific discoveries had been made in the 1700s and 1800s, many "modernist" thinkers believed that man could discover all that he needed to know to improve society without revelation from God. In the 1900s, two destructive world wars made the promises of ever greater progress in modernism far less believable. What would society's thinkers do? Would they see the failure of man to guide himself and turn to God for truth? No. Instead of accepting God's truth they would turn in the opposite direction and deny much of truth itself. That led to postmodernism.

Postmodernism tends to reject the idea of objective truth – that is, that certain facts are always true for everyone. It also rejects the idea that certain standards of morality are true for everyone. We will see more about the rejection of truth in the *next lesson*.

- What effect would a postmodern belief system would have upon a belief in the Bible?

- How do passages such as **Matthew 28:18-20** (known as the Great Commission) argue against the belief that there is no absolute truth and what is truth for one group at one time might not be truth for other groups at other times?

A second set of beliefs that affects many people today could be called **secularism**. This philosophy has many forms, but, for our purposes, we can think about it as the effort to remove religious beliefs and principles from government and public life. I do not want the church to run the government, but the determination to exclude all Christian beliefs from public life has some very dangerous consequences. This belief provides an excuse for many people to have no concern for the beliefs or principles of others. People who promote secularism may live as if man's opinions and the things of this world are the only things that matter or should even be discussed. Dealing with problems in society influenced by secular beliefs and values is the main topic of the ninth through twelfth lessons in our series.

- Can you see what this mindset would do to any concerns about faith?

- Corinth was a Greek city. The Greek way of thinking has continued to influence our culture almost 2000 years after the writing of this letter. What did Paul say that the Greeks wanted and how did he say that they regarded the gospel message in **1 Corinthians 1:18-25**?

- Many people say, "You can't legislate morality." In the sense that you cannot make people be more virtuous and conscientious just by passing laws, that often could be true. However, some people use that statement to claim that laws should not be made about moral issues, and that is clearly not true. Can you think of some laws that every society must make that involve punishing immoral behavior?

- Stealing   - rape
- lying

The third component of this worldview can infect even people who would reject the more extreme forms of the first two: **worldliness**. If we are concerned more with accumulating wealth and possessions or with being popular in this world rather than being right with God, we have a worldly attitude and we will not please God. Satan tries to get us to have this attitude without realizing it.

People do not have to believe that there is no God (atheism; see Psalm 14:1) to act as if there is no God (Psalm 10:3-4; Romans 1:28-32).

How should we respond to the world around us when it is opposed to truth and faith in so many ways? Christians have been dealing with this problem since the days of the apostles. The New Testament tells us how to handle it. Avoiding worldliness in common problem areas is the main topic of the *third through eighth* lessons in our series.

- According to **Titus 2:11-12**, what must we deny within ourselves to live for Christ? What must our attitude be? vs14 Zealous for good works

  denying ungodliness
  & worldly lusts
  - live soberly
  - righteously

- According to **1 Peter 4:1-2**, what must we be willing to do in this world if we want to be pleasing to God?

  do not live in the flesh and in lusts

- According to **Jude 17-19**, why would these "mockers" in the church divide people and lead them astray?

  they live in the flesh
  they lust for power

Christians are told to be "in the world, but not of the world" (as in 1 John 2:15-16). When we see what is happening in the world and some reasons why those things are happening we will be better equipped to resist temptation and live the way God wants us to live.

- What does **Romans 12:1-2** show us that we can do to avoid being conformed to (shaped to be like) this world?

  renew mind every day

5

Lesson 2
The Rejection of Objective Truth

Christ is rea

In the *first lesson,* we spoke of the philosophy of postmodernism. You might not have known the word, but you should know the way of thinking that explains some trends in our society. Postmodernism sees truth as a function of power. One conclusion some people draw from that is that if you are not in power, you don't have to accept facts or beliefs that you do not like because truth is subjective, something you determine for yourself. However, the Bible teaches that truth is **objective**, which means that the truth of a statement or belief is not affected by how any person feels or what any person thinks about it.

- A belief that facts are not absolute is going to cast doubt upon the reliability of history as well. Can you think of ways that the Bible uses historical fact to demonstrate the truth of its teaching?

  -David and temple   -gladiators, beasts
  - pharohs   to devour Christians

- What did Pilate ask in front of Jesus in **John 18:37-38**? If Pilate had really wanted to know the answer, would Jesus have told him?

  Evidence widespread of flood Genesis

  yes.

Many people today seem to welcome any belief except one that takes a strong stand against what is sinful. In connection with that, such people have the attitude that no one has the right to disapprove of what others are doing. This kind of thinking is inconsistent: If you are accusing people of doing wrong because they have told others that they are wrong about something, your criticism contradicts itself.

Andrew Tate, Spiritual leader?

In addition to being inconsistent in applying their statements about truth, people who think that truth is subjective tend not to think that truth is so subjective when they have signed a contract or when other people treat them in a way they consider unfair.

- The philosophers in Athens in **Acts 17:18-21** welcomed hearing about many different beliefs. Through the rest of the chapter Paul dealt with the inconsistency of some of their beliefs and told them what would truly honor God. What did Paul tell them to do and why **(17:30-31)**? What was the reaction most of his hearers had **(17:32-34)**?

  Repent for judgement comes
  "I'll hear you again about this"

Some people who claim to be Christians adopt part of that belief without realizing it. They might say things like, "I don't think it matters what you believe (as long as you believe in something)." They may speak of many different roads to Heaven, or say that there is some truth in every religion. When they say these kinds of things, they are arguing, often unintentionally, against the reality of absolute truth.

- According to **Psalm 119:160**, is accepting only some of the Bible as true acceptable? *Thy word is true from the beginning; and everyone from thy righteous judgements endures forever*

- What should the teaching in **1 John 5:20** indicate about the claims of Christianity to people who would say that all religions are equally true? *"This is the true God and eternal life"*

Not only is there objective truth, it can be understood.

- How did Paul say that the people who were receiving his letter in **Ephesians 3:3-4** could know what God wanted them to know about Christ? *Paul received by revelation, and they would understand the mystery of Christ*

- What does **Proverbs 2:1-5** tell us that we should do to understand what God wants us to know?
  - incline ear unto wisdom
  - apply heart to understanding

We can know that God is real, that He has created the world, and that His word is true.

- What does **Romans 1:18-20** tell us that all people should be able to understand about God by looking at the world and the universe around them? *God's handiwork is clearly seen*

- What is the source of the truth we can have in **John 1:14, 17**?
  Jesus Christ - WORD MANIFEST grace, truth

- What was the problem with the people in **2 Thessalonians 2:9-12** who believed things about God that were not true?
  - they pleasured in unrighteousness

- Some people think that the Bible is impossible to understand, or that people are unable to understand the Bible alike (which is different than saying that people might disagree about the Bible when they interpret it incorrectly). If that were true, what would that indicate about God, according to **1 Timothy 2:3-4**?

indicates God is uncaring, does not care about people

Objective truth exists and God makes it possible for us to understand it. Considering and accepting His truth allows us to understand all that we need to know to be right with Him. Please think about these things as we continue with the rest of the lessons in this series.

in marriage

I COR. 7:4 the body belongs to wife, husbands body belongs to wife

"Addiction is not a moral weakness"

Lesson 3
The Rejection of Responsibility

[handwritten: don't need repentance prayer and seek the Lord, go to our rehabilitation facility"]

When a group of people rejects the absolute truth of God's word as a standard for right and wrong behavior and elevates its own feelings as a standard (as in *the previous lesson*), you can expect many problems to result. One such problem in our society is that people have invented other explanations for unacceptable actions instead of calling sin what it is. Especially in the last few decades, worldly people have tried to classify behavior that hurts other people or damages other people's property as a sickness instead of a sin.[1]

- Can you think of examples of wrong and hurtful behavior that is sometimes called a sickness instead of a sin in our society? How do those things differ from the conditions that are usually called diseases?

  Anger/wrath → murder   looting → loss of business
  drug Abuse   Alchohol + drug addiction

- What are some other excuses that people might give when they claim that their own actions are not really their own fault?

- We cannot know exactly what the first man had in mind when explaining his sin to God; whom did Adam mention prominently when questioned about his sin by the LORD in **Genesis 3:10-12**?

  "the woman thou gavest me"

Some mental health professionals and other "experts" have even rejected the idea of self-control entirely, saying it is practically impossible for people to control their own behavior.

- How had some of the members of the church in Corinth changed themselves after having become Christians (**1 Corinthians 6:9-11**)?

  but ye are washed, ye are sanctified, but ye are justified in the name of the LORD Jesus.

- What did Peter say Christians should add (after knowledge) to their faith in **2 Peter 1:6**?

  And to Knowledge temperance.

1 COR. 9:25

I have read a few articles about a particular doctor who was one of the first to specialize in treating addiction. He researched treatments that helped people deal with the effects of withdrawal. That was a worthy pursuit. He also used his influence to turn many doctors away from a "punitive and moralistic approach" to addiction.[2] That means he and others saw addiction not as a matter of right or wrong (morality) and they also discouraged punishment for addicts. That pursuit was not so worthy. The New Testament describes how to deal with sinful behavior; God's plan includes serious negative consequences but also love and help for the sinner.

- In **1 Corinthians 5:1-5**, what did Paul say the church was to do when one of its members was involved in obvious sin and would not repent?

fornication, to deliver such a one to Satan. be removed

- What were the Corinthians specifically supposed to do to show their fellow Christian in sin that what he was doing was unacceptable (**1 Corinthians 5:9-13**)?

do not keep company with one who calls himself a Brother

- We do not know that the man discussed in **2 Corinthians 2:5-8** was the same one discussed in 1 Corinthians 5, but the same lessons should apply to this man whether he was the man in 1 Corinthians 5 or not. What were the Corinthians commanded to do for the sinner who had shown sorrow for his sin?

forgive and comfort

- If Paul described these kinds of situations in the church in Corinth, we might encounter them in the church today. What are some examples of problems that could come today when some try to tolerate sin instead of responding to it in the New Testament way?

a group can play the hipocrit

- Why should we be gentle when going to another Christian and trying to help him correct his sin (**Galatians 6:1-2**)?

restore in a manner of meekness, considering thyself, lest thyself be tempted

Some people face extremely difficult circumstances that make temptations very strong. Even those difficulties do not remove their responsibility to

James 4:8-10 Draw near to God and He will draw near to you. prayer be honest and just.

- What circumstances did the man in **Proverbs 6:30-31** face that made the temptation to steal very strong? What would he need to do when caught despite his desperate situation?

  hunger... stoles bread
  when found restores 7-fold, all substance of his house

Often the problem when people are involved in continuing sin (including addictions) is not a lack of ability to change, but a lack of desire to change.

- How did the people of Judah respond to the LORD's call to change in **Jeremiah 18:11-12**?

  "There is no hope; but we will walk after our own devices, and we will every one do the imagination of his evil heart"

The Bible makes clear that admitting our sins without trying to make excuses or blame others is <u>key to being forgiven and overcoming sin.</u>

- What two things from **Proverbs 28:13** must be done to receive mercy from God after we have sinned?

  He that <u>covereth</u> his sins shall not prosper: but whoso confesseth and forsaketh them shall have mercy.

- List some of the things that the Psalmist did when confessing his sin to the LORD in **Psalm 51:2-4** that showed he was truly repenting.

  "I acknowledge my transgressions."
  "I admit I struggle with this sin"

- When David admitted his adultery and his related sins to Nathan the prophet in **2 Samuel 12:13**, we do not read of his blaming others. Was anyone else involved in his sin that he might have tried to blame?

  Stress of running a kingdom
  Bathsheba, bathing outdoor naked

- In the Parable of the Prodigal Son, what had the son confessed before the father treated him with <u>mercy and generosity</u> (**Luke 15:21**)?

  "I have sinned against heaven and before thee
  I am not worthy"

Ezra learned that many of the Jews who had returned from exile had married women that God's law said they should not have married. He faced the unenviable task of leading the people in breaking up the sinful marriages (see this in the *sixteenth lesson*). He exercised a positive self-control and helped the Jewish people do right again.

- What did one of his fellow Jews tell him in **Ezra 10:4** to encourage him to faithfully complete his task?

  Arise; for this matter belongeth unto thee, we also
  will be with thee: be of good courage and do it.

Your responsibilities may not be as difficult as Ezra's, and I hope that you never sin in such a way as to cause as much widespread damage as David did. In any event, whatever your responsibility from God might be, fulfill it! Whatever sin you might commit, confess and forsake it! Accept the responsibilities God has given you and live for Him!

* discord
* Snap chat

God always wants to be #1
"I will wake the dawn the praises"

Prov. 30:15

Lesson 4
The Expectation of Instant Everything

The horseleech has 2 daughters: give and give.

We live in a time in which, for many people:

▶ four minutes to heat a meal in the microwave seems like far too long;

▶ pouring cereal and milk in a bowl for breakfast and eating it by the spoonful seems way too time-consuming;

▶ ordering anything we want online and waiting more than two days (if that) for it to arrive at the door seems impossibly slow;

▶ and getting a new smartphone that will download megabytes of data much faster than the one bought about two years ago seems like a necessity rivaling food and water in importance.

While wanting to have things quickly is not in itself wrong, we face the dangers of **impatience** (not being willing to wait) and **materialism** (living as if this life and this world are what matters most).

Patience is a quality that appears to be rare in our society. Politicians try to get elected by promising quick prosperity; not surprisingly, they can find soon themselves voted out of office by a fickle public when the economy seems a bit uncertain. In sports, players and coaches might find themselves praised everywhere after a good season but out of a job quickly after a bad one. Celebrities seem to rise and fall in the public consciousness based on their most recent work. Anyone who wants to please God must pursue patience (*1 Timothy 6:11*). *Flee love of money. Follow after patience*

· According to **Ecclesiastes 7:8**, the patient person is better than whom?

Better is the end of a thing than the beginning thereof: and the patient in spirit is better than the Proud in Spirit

· Patience is also key to spiritual growth in many ways. In the Parable of the Sower, what were the people represented by the good ground able to do because of patience (**Luke 8:15**)?

bring forth good fruit with patience

· In **James 1:3**, what produces patience in us? In **James 1:4**, what does patience do for us?

The trying of my faith

13

And having food and raiment let us be content

- What does patience allow faithful people to receive in **Hebrews 6:12, 15?**

  inherit the promises - eternal life
  heaven

- According to **Romans 15:4-5**, what does the patience of the Scriptures allow us to have?

  to have hope
  likeminded one toward another according
  to Christ Jesus

Being too eager to get more money or other material things causes spiritual problems.

- For what did the younger son in the Parable of the Prodigal Son ask and what did he do with it once he had it **(Luke 15:11-13)**?

  give me the portion of goods that falls to me.
  ★ wasted his substance with riotous living

It is easy for a desire to have more things more quickly to become greed. The love of money causes all kinds of sin and leads some to turn away from faith in Christ (_1 Timothy 6:9-10_).

- According to **Proverbs 1:19**, what can greed do to a person who is greedy?

  So are the ways of everyone that
  is greedy of gain; which taketh away
  the life of the owners thereof

- In **Proverbs 21:25-26**, what does a righteous person do instead of being lazy and greedy?

  the righteous giveth and spareth not

- Which groups of Christians are forbidden to be greedy in **1 Timothy 3:3, 8** and **Titus 1:7**?

  An elder, a bishop   not greedy of filthy
  lucre

Closely related to greed is <u>covetousness</u>, which includes the idea of wanting what other people have. It is possible, in a society so afflicted with instant gratification, for the desire to have something now to grow <u>into the desire to take those things from others.</u>

- In the last of the Ten Commandments (**Exodus 20:17**), what are the things that Israel was forbidden to covet?

  - house
  - wife
  - manservant , maidservant
  - ox or donkey
  - nor anything that is your neighbors

- Why did Jesus warn His listeners to watch out for covetousness in **Luke 12:13-15?**

  for a mans life consisteth not in the a

- Jesus followed the warning about covetousness with the Parable of the Rich Fool (**Luke 12:16-21**). Was it necessarily wrong for a successful farmer to plan to build bigger barns? If not, what was the spiritual problem?

  Soul is concerned with goods over the Spirit.

  "Thou fool, this night thy soul shall be required of thee   his goal: treasure for self

- Why was the Rich Fool condemned at the end of that parable?

  his soul was required of him and he was not rich towards God

- According to **Hebrews 13:5**, which attitude should we have instead of covetousness? What has the Lord said that allows us to have that attitude?

  Let your conversation be without covetousness and be content with such things as ye have: for he hath said, I will never leave thee, nor forsake thee.

We can fight the desire to have everything right away by working on becoming content with the things that we have. This includes material possessions, as *1 Timothy 6:6-8* shows us, but it also helps us be patient when we want God to do things for us.

  But godliness with contentment is great gain.

- What kinds of things are we told not to worry about in **Matthew 6:25-26, 33-34?**

  food, drink, clothing, tomorrow

- After Paul had written of how he could be content with little or much, who did he say had allowed him to do everything that he needed to do (**Philippians 4:11-13**)?

  I can do all things through Christ which Strengtheneth me.

- What did Paul say to do in **Philippians 4:6-7** to keep us from being anxious and to help us have the peace of God?

  * by prayer and supplication with thanksgiving let your requests be made known to God.

Instead of always wanting everything right away, like so many people around us, we should be sure to be thankful for and content with what we already have. That helps us fight greed and covetousness.

15

Lesson 5
The Expectation of Receiving Everything for Free

In our society, we have certain freedoms (though those freedoms were and are secured at great cost). No one can take away our freedoms unless we have misused them to break the law, hurt other people, or damage their property. We also expect some services in society to be free. We do not want the police to demand payment from victims before investigating the crimes that have hurt them. We do not want firefighters to put out fires only for those wealthy enough to pay them well.

The popular expectations of what should be free have expanded over time. Sometimes politicians seem to compete to see who can promise voters the most free things. Of course, the things promised are not really free – someone else will be paying for others to receive them without cost. A feeling of **entitlement**, that one is owed help and support from others to obtain what is needed or desired, can be dangerous.

The Bible commands Christians to care for those in need (1 John 3:17). The Bible commands Christians to be a giving people (Matthew 5:42). At the same time, the Bible commands each of us to do what we can to support ourselves and help others.

We Can Choose To Give to and Serve Others for Christ's Sake

Instead of keeping our focus on what we want to receive and how we should be served, we should think first of what we can give (Acts 20:35) and how we can serve others (Mark 10:45; Luke 22:26-27).

- What should we be willing to do for others because of what Jesus has done for us (**John 13:13-15**)?

  wash one anothers feet

- What was Nehemiah's attitude toward what he could have received for himself as the governor of the land in **Nehemiah 5:14-15**?

  he did not rule with an iron fist nor take money from people nor eat food provided

We Need To Be Willing To Support Ourselves

No shame should result from needing help. We all come into this life needing others to take care of us and many of us will leave it in a

16

similar way. Many people do not have the ability to provide for all of their own needs and we should gladly help them. However, to the extent that we can provide for our own needs, we should want to do so.

- If the Christians in Thessalonica who were receiving **1 Thessalonians** would "work with their hands" (**4:11**), what would they be able to do (**4:12**)?

  walk honestly

- In **Ephesians 4:28**, why was the person who had stolen things in the past told to work?

  that he may have to give to needy

- While Paul could be fully supported financially in his work of preaching (1 Corinthians 9), he sometimes worked in other ways to help support himself. Why did Paul say he had worked to support himself in **2 Thessalonians 3:7-9**?

  labor and travail night and day
  -not chargeable to any, to be an example

- What did Paul say about those Christians in Thessalonica who were unwilling to work at all in **2 Thessalonians 3:10-12**?

  neither should he/she eat

- What temptations did Paul say could be faced by widows if they were still young enough to have new families but were having all of their financial needs met by the church (**1 Timothy 5:11-14**)?

  idle, wandering house to house, tattlers
  + busybodies

- In **1 Timothy 5:16**, who had the first responsibility to support a widowed Christian: her family members or the congregation?

  Sons + daughters

We Must Give What We Have To Serve God

We should not think of ourselves as only receiving good things from God. Real sacrifice and real service involves our giving and must cost us something personally.

- When David was told to build an altar to the LORD on Araunah's threshing floor, Araunah offered to give David the threshing floor and the items to sacrifice at no cost (**2 Samuel 24:22-24**). Why did

17

David refuse?

- In the Parable of the Minas, one servant did nothing at all with the mina his master had given him, simply returning it to the master (**Luke 19:20-26**). How did his master regard him? How could we apply this lesson to our service to God? *question compares*

" *wicked servant* " → *fiscal / physical money wealth*
  # lazy   → *spiritual gains*

God Gives Freely

? double negatives triple negative → positive

To say that we should not feel entitled to have all of our needs provided for us should not make us think that we earn God's blessings. To say that we must obey God to please Him, to be forgiven, and to be saved should not make us think that His merciful gift is any less free.

- Paul speaks about the free gift that came through the sacrifice of Jesus Christ in **Romans 5:15-18**. What can people have as a result of that free gift in 5:16?

free gift → justification of life
in judgement this offense would have led to condemnation

- What will those who receive this gracious gift have in Romans 5:17?

life

- According to **Matthew 20:26-28**, Jesus' purpose in coming to earth was not to have others serve Him (in the sense of taking care of His physical needs as a slave would). Why did He come to earth?

but to minister and to give his life as ransom for many.

God has freely given us every spiritual blessing in Christ (Ephesians 1:3). We need to respond to His infinitely great blessings by serving God and serving other men. We need to respond to His giving by giving to others as we have opportunity. *women* Putting ourselves first and expecting others to always give to us and serve us only leads to unhappiness and spiritual failure.

ransom - a sum of money or other payment demanded or paid for release of a prisoner

Lesson 6
The Expectation of Never Being Uncomfortable

Many people in our society do not want to deal with words or ideas that are unpleasant to them. While this desire has always been present, a few changes have made avoiding what is unpleasant or uncomfortable easier to achieve:

▶ You can find many websites and often entire television networks dedicated to presenting mostly or entirely things with which you already agree. These are available for almost every point of view. Sometimes these are called "echo chambers."

▶ Some universities and other groups are promoting "trigger warnings," in which anything likely to be uncomfortable for certain groups is noted ahead of time.

▶ Some groups promote "safe spaces," in which expressing anything negative about that group is forbidden.

Not all of these things are always wrong. You probably enjoy spending some of your time with like-minded friends. We should all want to be sensitive to the concerns of others, especially those who have suffered abuse. However, much of the way this is practiced in our society today is one-sided. Do literature classes issue trigger warnings for profane and blasphemous books? I would appreciate that, but those concerns are usually ignored. Do many universities concern themselves with respecting a viewpoint consistent with Biblical morality and the beliefs of those who oppose sexual immorality and promote marriage between one man and one woman? Usually not; sometimes those people are labeled "hateful" and "bigoted" instead. The kind of safe space described above is usually reserved for those who demand that other people "respect" or "tolerate" (more accurately termed "approve of") their lifestyles, which violate Biblical teaching.

The Bible tells of people who did not want to hear what was unpleasant because they desired to follow their own will instead of God's will. We look at the Biblical examples of this problem and the solution.

Wanting To Hear Only What Pleases You

Many people only want to hear things that are positive or things with

19

which they already agree. This is often true of politics and often also true when it comes to religion.

- What did many of the children of Israel want the prophets to tell them in **Isaiah 30:9-11**?

  Children that will not hear the law of the LORD seers - see not phophets - dont tell us right things tell us easy things to hear

- Some Christians today expect preachers to speak of only positive things in their sermons. What are some dangers of that approach?

  the law is not addressed and the people sin

- How did many of the people of Judah feel about the false prophets and the ungodly priests in **Jeremiah 5:30-31**?

  they loved it to have it so

- How will a righteous person eventually feel about someone who rebukes him for the right reason (**Proverbs 28:23**)?

  more favor

- Why did the false teachers of **Jude 16** flatter Christians?

  having men's persons in admiration because of advantage

Not Wanting To Hear What Does Not Please You

Some people refuse to hear what they do not want to hear, no matter how true or necessary the message is.

- How did King Ahab of Israel feel about the prophet Micaiah, who told him the hard truth (**1 Kings 22:7-8**)?

  "but I hate him"

- What did the Jewish Council (Sanhedrin) do immediately before running to stone Stephen when he had told them the truth about Jesus and their response to Him (**Acts 7:55-58**)?

  Stopped their ears

- What was the problem with the Hebrew Christians' hearing in **Hebrews 5:11**? What effect did it have on them (**5:12-14**)?

  hard to be uttered, they were dull of hearing

→ unskillfull in the word of righteousness → they are wanting

Finding People Who Will Say Only What Pleases You

Some people find popularity by telling people what they want to hear and not what they need to hear.

· What did the false prophets say to those who paid or fed them in **Micah 3:5**? What did they say to those who did not feed them?

false prophets said "peace" to those who fed them
★ prepare war against those who do not feed them

· According to **2 Timothy 4:2-4**, what kind of preaching would many insincere Christians demand?

heap to themselves teachers after their own lusts

· What kinds of promises will many politicians make in order to get elected? Can you see any similarities to what we have already studied?

- lower gas prices
- better economy (more jobs)
- Free healthcare

The Methods of False Teachers

False teachers often find an audience by telling people what they want to hear, especially when they tell people that they do not have to do the difficult and painful things that God's word says are necessary to help those in sin.

· What had the false prophets told the people of Judah in **Jeremiah 14:13-14**?
- no war will come
- no hunger
- assured peace

· How did the false teachers deceive Christians in **Romans 16:17-18**? Whom were the false teachers really serving?

divisions and offenses contrary to the doctrine → they serve their own belly

· What would the false teachers use to try to deceive Christians in **Colossians 2:4, 8**?

- enticing words
- philosophy or vain deceit

Standing for What Is Right

Speaking the truth for the cause of Christ means that we must be willing to stand against opposition. Both testaments are full of examples of those who loved others enough to speak even when it was hard. We must not run away from controversy or be intimidated into silence by our opponents.

- What are Christians told to be ready to give to those who ask them about their hope in **1 Peter 3:15**?

  an answer in meekness and fear

- According to **Ephesians 4:15**, how must we speak the truth to others?

  in love

What Jesus Did When Faced with the Wrong Advice

Jesus boldly spoke the truth to those who opposed Him. He also told the hard truth to His followers when they were speaking in a way that was not right.

- When Peter tried to convince Jesus not to suffer and die in the way that was necessary, apparently thinking that he was being helpful, what did Jesus say to him (**Matthew 16:21-23**)?

  ★ Get thee behind me Satan
  ★ thou art an offense unto me

Those who attempt to discourage others from doing what is necessary but difficult may think that they are helping others be safe, but in reality they are tempting others to forsake true service and growth.

Be willing to seek and listen to the truth and then do what it says, no matter how inconvenient.

Lesson 7
Social Media

Social media (Facebook, Instagram, and similar sites and applications) can be a wonderful way to stay in touch with friends and family far away, sharing the important events in their lives and yours. People can be encouraged and prayers can be multiplied when it is used well.

Even a slight familiarity with social media exposes you to its dark side. People can parade their evil desires before others. Evil people can find potential victims. Searching social media can be a horrifying experience. Evil influences can be multiplied through its abuse.

Social media has not caused new forms of evil to be invented; it has amplified the temptations with which people have long struggled, making bad things easy to find anywhere and anytime. We will be covering the problems with the **content** of social media and other forms of entertainment in *upcoming lessons* (profanity, pornography, and sensuality).

This leads to a problem: It is easy to link to or promote sites or video clips that are ungodly; Christians have thoughtlessly shared inappropriate content and caused harm by doing so. Not only can the sharing take place worldwide, but it is often very hard to fully remove an unwise comment or a harmful picture placed online. Many people have lost their influence or their jobs because of something placed on social media long before.

A more subtle problem that often comes with social media is the tendency to become obsessed with attention. The temptation to seek attention and praise in a sinful way is not new, but social media makes it easier. Many people spend large amounts of time seeking attention from others for their pictures, posts, and comments in a way that resembles addiction. Christians must not be obsessed with getting other people to notice and praise them as individuals, but work on reflecting the glory of God to the world around them.

Example: supporting an artist auction ★ *Ukraine* ★ *stop school shooting* ★ *abortion?*

Not Approving Sinful Things

When we "like" or approve the wrong things we hurt ourselves and often hurt others.

- What kinds of things ought we to approve (**Philippians 1:9-11**),
  - *excellent*
  - *glorifies God, praises God*
  - *without offense to Christ*

23

whether in person or online?

- According to **Matthew 18:5-6**, what would be better than causing a little one to sin?

  millstone be hung around one's neck and cast into the sea

- **Matthew 5:28-30** teaches us that it would be better, if necessary, to remove an eye or a hand rather than let temptation destroy us spiritually. What application could we make to being tempted to watch evil things on social media?

  - removes those apps!
  - take internet off one's phone

Being an Influence for Good

If we keep the right attitude, we can be an influence for good with our online presence. Righteous people are the kind of social media "influencers" we really need.

- After reading **Matthew 5:14-16** and **Philippians 2:14-16**, list some ways to be a light in the online world.

  let your light so shine before men that they may see your good works and glorify your Father in heaven/midst of crooked + perverse generation

- How does **Colossians 4:5-6** instruct us to react online to someone who has disagreed with or criticized us?

  grace, seasoned with salt that ye may know how to answer each person

- Many people think (often incorrectly) that no one online knows who they are and they use social media to harshly criticize others. Some people share gossip and criticism with those whom they know online. What does **1 Thessalonians 4:9-12** tell us about these practices?

  be quiet and do own business

Not Promoting Ourselves Sinfully

Many people seek to promote themselves, getting more followers online. They feed on others' attention and approval.

- According to **Philippians 2:3-4**, whose interests ought we to seek in what we do?

  Let nothing be done through strife or vainglory

- As we see in **2 Corinthians 10:12, 18**, even those who preach and teach the gospel could hurt themselves by comparing themselves with others. Whose approval should we really seek?

Do not compare ourselves with those that brag about themselves — this is not wise! measure of the rule which God has distributed to us.

Putting Others First

The Bible consistently teaches us to move our focus from serving ourselves to serving others.

- Read the description of what love does in **1 Corinthians 13:4-7**. How many phrases can you find that deal with not seeking attention and not being selfish? *does not show off*
  does not think too highly of itself
  puts the other first

- Paul praised Timothy in **Philippians 2:20-22** because he did not put his own interests first, unlike many people. What had Timothy done instead? *Most people! Seek their own, not the things of Christ Jesus / Timothy cared for others!*

- **Philippians 1:15-17** describes some men who preached with evil motives while Paul was in prison. What did Paul say about how they were doing that?

Not Boasting

Sometimes people like to boast about themselves and their experiences on social media.

- What do **Proverbs 25:27** and **27:2** teach us about how we should regard ourselves?
  ★for men to search their own glory is not not glory "Let another praise thee and not thy own mouth, a stranger and not thy own Lips

- According to **Galatians 5:26**, what might we do to others if we become conceited or proud?
  Provoking one another
  envying one another

- **James 3:14-16** warns us twice against envy (or jealousy) and another evil tendency. What is that?

brag and lie (hypocrisy?)

25

The fruit of righteousness is sown in peace of them that make peace

- To live honorably among others in the world and to protect our own souls, from what must we abstain (**1 Peter 2:11-12**)?

~~worldly~~ lusts
fleshly

Make sure your online presence and activities glorify God instead of yourself. Use the digital world as a tool for good instead of evil.

- Share Bible verses
- advertise for a good cause

Lesson 8
The Expectation of Continual Entertainment

Our society has a problem distinguishing between joy and happiness. Too many people seek short-term worldly happiness instead of long-lasting spiritual joy. This is seen in the attitude most people have toward entertainment and the way they seem to expect to be entertained constantly.

> "By 2016, the average 12th grader said they spent a staggering six hours a day texting, on social media, and online during their free time."[3] – Jean Twenge

While the exact numbers vary from study to study, what is clear is that many teens spend hours daily watching screens, and school assignments and work likely represent only a small part of that time. How many opportunities for good (serving God and learning about Him) are lost?

- What does it mean to be "redeeming the time" in **Ephesians 5:15-16**? Consider the context.
  - making good use of time
  - not wasting time

Much of Popular Entertainment Is Ungodly

Our *next few lessons* will examine the character of much of the popular entertainment in America today. At one time, most entertainment (though not all) had far less bad language and explicit content. At one time, attitudes that dishonored God and His moral standards were rarely shown positively in television shows and movies. That time has passed, and Christians need to actively seek entertainment that contains proper values, not just go along with whatever is popular. If we consume a lot of popular entertainment, we are probably consuming a lot of evil influence with it and being affected more than we realize.

- **Psalm 1:1-3** teaches us that thinking about godly things helps us grow spiritually. What should we expect if we spend much of our time filling our minds with things that are not good?

we will become ungodly, sinners and scorn the way

Purposeless Entertainment Cannot Make Us Truly Happy

An overemphasis on entertainment is connected with materialism. Many people spend a tremendous amount of money on cable bills, subscriptions to various forms of media, and tickets for movies, sports, and concerts. Today we can gain access to a great deal on entertainment without (directly) spending money by watching videos online, but that does not eliminate the danger. If we spend ~~more~~ *more* money on entertainment but pay more attention to entertaining ourselves than following the Lord and helping others, we will become poor in the only ways that matter.

- According to **Proverbs 14:13**, what could someone who is laughing on the outside be feeling on the inside?

  Even in laughter the heart is sorrowful, and the end of that mirth is heaviness

- What did the Preacher (almost certainly Solomon), the writer of **Ecclesiastes**, test in **2:1-2**? What was his conclusion?

  parable of sower

  Pleasure = vanity   laughter = madness
  mirth = what is its purpose?

List the kinds of entertainment mentioned in **Ecclesiastes 2**:

⭐

- **2:3** ■ *give self to alcohol/drink + wisdom*

- **2:4-6** *great works: houses, vineyards, orchards*

- **2:8** *our senses are never satisfied*
  "the eye is not satisfied with seeing nor the ear filled with hearing

- What was the Preacher's conclusion in **Ecclesiastes 2:10-11** after having surveyed all of these things?

  vanity and vexation of spirit and no profit under the sun

The Preacher also had some things to say about indulging in entertainment in **Ecclesiastes 7:1-6**:

vanity - excessive pride in self or one's accomplishments

- What is more valuable than spending time feasting (7:2)? Why?

  go to the house of mourning

- What is better than laughter, and who lives in the "house of mirth" (7:3-4)?   *Sorrow*
  heart of fools

Forrest in Japan

- What is better than the song of fools, and what does the laughter of fools sound like (7:5-6)?

  ★ *rebuke of the wise*

28

"crackling of thorns under a pot

Entertainment Is Not Always Evil, But Work and Service Is Our Purpose

Some people act as if the whole purpose of their existence is to be entertained. Christians' real purpose is to work for and serve the Lord. Many churches need to be reminded of their true purpose. Some downplay serious worship and emphasize entertainment to draw visitors and keep members. Some have false teachers that please members by telling them what they want to hear (2 Timothy 4:2-4). Congregations must be careful to worship only as God has authorized; 1 Corinthians 11:22-34 shows how erring Christians had changed the Lord's Supper from a holy observance into a social meal, which had also changed its purpose and appeal.

Free Food

All of us need recreation, but life offers much more that is good and lasting than most popular entertainment. A life centered around serving God will be truly satisfying.

- What did the Preacher of Ecclesiastes say is our purpose, and why is it our purpose (**Ecclesiastes 12:13-14**)?

  Fear God and keep His commandments for this is the whole duty of man

- In the Parable of the Rich Fool (**Luke 12:13-21**), what did the prosperous man want to do with his abundance (12:19)?

  "take thine ease; eat, drink and be merry.

- Much entertainment in our society is profane, explicit, and irreverent. What does **Titus 2:11-12** say teaches us to oppose such things? What does **2:13-14** teach us to want instead?

  Looking for that blessed hope → teaches us to deny ungodliness
  when we remember Jesus died for our sins

- What did Paul seek instead of his own profit (**1 Corinthians 10:31-33**)?   *- give no offense to anyone*

  Seeking not my own profit, but the profit of many that they may be saved

- What were we created in Christ Jesus to do (**Ephesians 2:10**)?

  good works

- What does God, who has called us to freedom (or liberty), want us to do (**Galatians 5:13-14**)?

  in love serve one another
  "Thou shalt love thy neighbor as thyself

29

Finding Real Joy Is the Alternative to Ungodly Entertainment

Please do not leave this lesson thinking that life is intended to be humorless or miserable. Sharing good experiences with friends is wonderful. Enjoying good things with family and friends is a blessing. Finding pleasure in the beautiful world that God has made is a gift from Him that He is glad for us to accept with gratitude. God wants us to enjoy those things, and even more than that He wants us to have real and lasting joy as the best kind of happiness. We can have joy when we are faithful to Christ.

· What did the Preacher say is a gift from God in **Ecclesiastes 5:18-20**?

> riches + wealth

· **Romans 14** speaks about how Christians who differ on nonessential matters (things that God has neither commanded nor forbidden, such as eating meat) should treat each other. What does **14:16-17** say that the kingdom of God is and is not?

> For the Kingdom of God is not meat
> + drink
> But → righteousness + peace + joy in

· What was John's great joy in **3 John 3-4?** the Holy Ghost

> thy children walk in truth,
> as we have recieved a commandment from the Father

It is when we remove God's goodness from the things that we find pleasing that we get in trouble. We take away the goodness from entertainment when we make the wrong choices about what to watch and hear and when we let ourselves be influenced by evil things in the entertainment we consume. We might treat worldly entertainment as an end in itself, only to find that it cannot keep its promise to make us happy. It is when we put God and serving Him first, letting acceptable entertainment find its proper place, that we find real joy.

> prayer
>
> Bonnie Kanatzar ~ virus
> Jesse · Jackie in automobile accident
>   Claire - Mr. Ruben's mother

Lesson 9

Profanity and Other Evil Speech

The word *profane* refers to things that are <u>unholy or irreverent</u>. We use a form of the word, **profanity**, to speak of bad language. Saying bad words or bad things about God is certainly profane, although that is not all that is called profane in the Bible. (Examples: unauthorized worship in Leviticus 10:1; theft in Proverbs 30:9; and violating the Sabbath in Ezekiel 20:21.)

Profane speech is probably the most common example of a profane act and it is all around us. It has become increasingly accepted in everyday speech; words that would have caused many people shock a few generations ago receive little notice now. Profanity is constant in many workplaces, especially when customers are not present.

Profanity is pervasive in media as well. Consider this quote:

> "Given that pretty much every modern song contains bad language …" - Rick Broida[4]

Profanity in First Ten Billboard Top 100 Songs for 2018[5]

Song	Artist(s)	Obscene	Sexual	Irreligious
God's Plan	Drake	3	1	0
Perfect	Ed Sheeran	0	0	0
Meant To Be	Bebe Rexha & Florida Georgia Line	0	0	0
Havana	Camila Cabello Featuring Young Thug	0	0	1
Rockstar	Post Malone Featuring 21 Savage	9	6	2
Psycho	Post Malone Featuring Ty Dolla $ign	5	2	0
I Like It	Cardi B, Bad Bunny, and J Balvin	10	3	2
The Middle	Zedd, Maren Morris, and Grey	0	1	0
In My Feelings	Drake	15	3	0
Girls Like You	Maroon 5 Featuring Cardi B	1	4	1

old country songs?

There are probably additional sexual references implied than directly stated in some of the songs, including the relatively clean songs. The numbers might not seem so high until you consider that the songs are only a few minutes long and played repeatedly.

Not only music, but also movies and video clips are full of bad language. Books and websites can be full of cursing and obscenity. The comments and even the usernames in multiplayer games are frequently full of profanity. In the *next lesson* we will look at the related problem of sensuality, which often runs rampant in visual forms of entertainment.

- Plays
- entertainment (gladiator coliseum) ~80 years old history of television 1940-1950

Profanity in Top-Grossing Movies of 2018-2019[6]

Insidious

Year	Gross ($Millions)	Name	Rating	Obscene	Anatomical	Irreligious
2018	$700	Black Panther	PG-13	5	5	0
	$679	Avengers: Infinity War	PG-13	11	15	9
	$609 •	Incredibles 2	PG	3	3	2
	$418	Jurassic World: Fallen ...	PG-13	5	10	12
	$335	Aquaman	PG-13	8	10	1
	$325	Deadpool 2	R	91	73	31
	$271 ⦁	Dr. Seuss' The Grinch	PG	0	0	1
	$220	Mission: Impossible ...	PG-13	11	10	10
	$217	Ant-Man and the Wasp	PG-13	19	5	9
	$216	Bohemian Rhapsody	PG-13	5	26	5
2019	$858	Avengers: Endgame	PG-13	8	22	8
	$544 •	The Lion King	PG	0	3	1
	$434 ⦁	Toy Story 4	G	0	0	0
	$427	Captain Marvel	PG-13	11	8	2
	$405 ⦁	Frozen II	PG	0	1	0
	$391 ✗ ⦁	Spider-Man: Far from ...	PG-13	10	7	6
	$356	Aladdin	PG	0	0	0
	$333	Joker	R	29	14	3
	$290	Star Wars: The Rise of ...	PG-13	6	1	0
	$212	It: Chapter Two	R	115	60	17

Please note that these counts are estimates and probably on the low side. Also, there are several reasons other than language (for instance, see the *next lesson*) why a movie may be a poor choice for viewing.

Using Evil Words

We will not be able to control the speech of everyone in the world around us. When we do have a choice about what we hear, why would we choose to fill our ears and minds with evil words and thoughts as entertainment? If these things should "not even be named among you" (see the next passage), why would we voluntarily pump those words and thoughts into our consciousness?

· Which of the sinful things that Paul lists in **Ephesians 5:3-5** involve profane language?
  filthiness, foolish talking, jesting

When we listen to a song, we should ask ourselves questions such as these:

▶ What do the lyrics of this song influence me and others to say and do?

▶ Does this song's attitude toward God help me to honor Him or keep me from honoring Him?

▶ Do I really want to be like the people who are portrayed in or are performing this song?

Do not be decieved!

Some people think that they are not affected by <u>the words and actions in movies and music.</u> In reality, it would be very strange if they were not affected. Words set to music are easy to remember and hard to forget. Words associated with graphic images will stick with us more than others. We should expect them to influence our choices, especially in unguarded moments where we may speak without much thinking.

You should not expect music streaming services to screen their songs effectively for all but perhaps the most offensive lyrics (if they offer content controls at all). You should expect them to allow many things in their screened songs that would still harm you spiritually.

We must not only avoid what is corrupt, but actively seek to say what is good.

· According to **Ephesians 4:29**, what will good language do for those who listen to us?

  — good to the use of edifying
  — minister grace to the hearer

Taking God's Name in Vain

Compared to some of the obscene things people say, using God's name (or a euphemism like "gosh" or an abbreviation like "OMG") might seem mild. The Bible makes clear that not respecting God's name enough to use it only in the proper way is a very serious matter.

★ · What does it mean to take God's name "in vain" as in **Exodus 20:7**? Explain it in your own words and list a few different ways that someone could sin by taking God's name in vain. *will not hold him guiltless*

· How were the people described who were taking God's name in vain in **Psalm 139:19-20**?

  wicked, bloody men.

Swearing and Using Oaths

Sometimes using bad language is called "swearing" even when the person using it is not making an oath. One of the ways that people misused God's name then and still misuse it now is to make it part of some statement where it does not belong. People who use God's name to "strengthen" a promise that they might not try to keep are misusing it. People who toss God's name casually into a promise without thinking about it are misusing it. People who use God's name to make a promise that they might be

" I swear to God "

unable to keep, even because of circumstances beyond their control, are misusing it.

- What did the LORD forbid the Israelites to do in **Leviticus 19:11-12**?

  Do not swear by my name falsely
  Do not profane the LORD

- How are we to speak so as to avoid falling into judgment in **James 5:12?** *lest you fall in to condemnation*
  let yes be yes and no be no

- What are the reasons given for not swearing oaths in **Matthew 5:33-37?** *swear not at all!*   *- nor Jeruselem, the great King*
  - by heaven, God's throne - nor thy head,
  - earth- God's footstool   we cannot turn a hair
  color on our own

Speaking against God   *- More than yea & nea is from evil or*

Bad language is not the only problem in common forms of entertainment. Much entertainment is created and produced by people who flagrantly disregard Biblical morality and are happy to say so. We could also be influenced by those people to think and believe things about God that are not true.

- What does a person who speaks evil things demonstrate about himself (**Matthew 12:34-35**)?

  for out of the abundance of the
  heart the mouth speaks

- How will our words be used in the day of judgment (**Matthew 12:36-37**)? *every idle word a man speaks they shall*
  give an account @ judgement; by thy words

Not Controlling Our Words *we are justified and condemned*

We need to control our words so that we do not speak in the sinful ways described above.

- According to **Matthew 15:18-20**, what can the things that we say do to us spiritually? From where do our words really come?
  - our speech can defile us (unholy)
  - out of the heart, things that truly defile

- Some people might claim that bad language is "just words" and does not show anything seriously wrong with their spiritual life. What does **James 3:6** teach about that idea?

tongue a fire, world of iniquity

- What does the Psalmist say that we should do to live a long and good life in **Psalm 34:12-13**?

tongue from evil, lips from speaking deceit

- What kind of act shows that a person's religion is useless in **James 1:26**?

Cannot tame the tongue

The Solution: Speaking in an Edifying Way

In addition to avoiding speaking in evil ways, we should also be careful to speak what is right.

- According to **Colossians 3:16-17**, what should guide all of our speech?

the WORD OF GOD

Make sure that what you say is consistent with what you sing, what you pray, and whatever other words you use in praise of God.

April 24th   cause   **Lesson 10**
                        clicks
                              Sensuality
            ★ Sexual things
            ★ gain
            ★ drama

Our society has a problem not only with the words it chooses to say (the *previous lesson*) but also with the images it chooses to see. Sensuality is the obsession with pleasing the senses; many things that are sensual appeal to what is seen and the appeals are driven by lust (the *next lesson*), but there are also other kinds of sensuality and other dangers. Your Bible translation might use words such as "uncleanness," "lasciviousness," or "lewdness" for sensuality.

Many popular forms of entertainment (such as music, television, and movies) are filled with sensuality. Before we listen to or watch something with any ungodly content, we should carefully consider questions such as these:

▶ Could I watch the immodesty in this movie and not be led to lust?

▶ Does the video I am watching influence me and others to do sinful or dangerous things?

▶ If Jesus were with me, would I want Him to see me being entertained by this?

Even things that we do not usually consider entertainment can be sources of ungodliness. Many commercials use sensuality to try to sell products, often by trying to link owning the product with fulfilling other desires. In this world, that frequently works for the advertisers. Many people think that their choices of what to buy are not affected in the least by advertisements; they are almost always wrong. Sensual advertisements can also affect us morally by tempting us to imitate the sinful things seen in them.

We Must Not Be Controlled by Lust

Many of the desires to please our senses are not always wrong; the problem is that people fall under the control of those desires and are willing to do sinful things to fulfill them instead of finding fulfillment in serving the Lord.

· The lives of many people are driven by sensual lusts. According to **1 Peter 4:1-5**, what should be the purpose of our lives instead of sensuality? instead of lust of flesh live for God's will

Jaydn

- Whom would we be rejecting by living an immoral life (**1 Thessalonians 4:7-8**)?

  God

- Sensuality makes our lives less useful and gradually makes us less able to understand and respond to what is good. What are some of the phrases in **Ephesians 4:17-19** that illustrate the deadening effect of sensuality? _Caloused + hardened of heart heathen_

- List some of the things that caused God to give up people to sensuality in **Romans 1:21-24**.

  Professing to be wise they became fools.

We Could Participate Unwittingly through What We Wear

Another kind of sensuality comes from popular fashions. Many of the clothes advertised and displayed prominently in stores and in their advertisements are too short, too low, too tight, or too thin (in the sense of transparent). While trends will vary over time, we have little reason to expect that in the next few years Christians will be able to buy and wear whatever is popular and be confident that it will not be immodest. We cannot let the world set our standards, especially now.

- In **Isaiah 47:1-3**, Babylon was pictured as a woman. What part of her body was uncovered that was a source of shame?

- There are several ways to be immodest besides not wearing enough clothing. In what way was the clothing criticized in **1 Timothy 2:9-10** immodest? _Shame facedness and sobriety; not with costly clothing but good works_   _propriety moderation_

We Can Take Steps To Repent of and Prevent Sensual Sin

God provides instruction about how to handle sensual desires and to repent of sins that we have committed (2 Corinthians 12:20-21).

- What were the readers of **1 Peter 1:13-16** supposed to do instead of returning to following sinful lusts as they had before learning the

  gird up the loins of your mind
  - do not be like before
  - be holy in all things

37

gospel?

Slaves to sin and iniquity

- To whom or to what had the readers of **Romans 6:16-19** been slaves when they had lived in ways that were sensual or unclean?

sin → death
obedience → righteousness

- How does **2 Corinthians 7:1** say that we should live after cleansing ourselves from sinful desires and actions?

Perfecting holiness in the fear of God

- How did Lot feel about the wickedness of Sodom (**2 Peter 2:7-8**)?

Vexed with the filthy conversation of the wicked

- When you look back at the bad things that happened to Lot in **Genesis 19**, how many of those things could be connected to the sensuality dominating life in Sodom and the effect that it may have had upon his family?

- daughters raped their father
- incest.

False Teaching Can Be Based on Sensuality

Some people are shocked when someone who does not teach the truth about God's word does not live according to the truth, but it should not be such a surprise. The Bible frequently connects error in teaching with sensuality in behavior.

- According to **2 Peter 2:18**, what do false teachers use to allure Christians to follow them instead of the truth?

Swelling words of vanity, allure through lust of the flesh

- Find at least one other place in 2 Peter 2 in which false teaching and sensual living are connected.

through covetousness vs. 3
eyes full of adultery; beguiling unstable souls vs. 14

- According to **Jude 4**, what had the false teachers changed into something sensual (or lewd or lascivious)? How could they have done that?

Grace of our God → lasciviousness
"reflecting or producing sexual desire or behavior"

- According to **Jude 18-19**, what were ungodly and sensual teachers causing in the church?

  division

In our next lesson we will continue studying what the Bible says about sensuality in one of its most extreme forms.

Pluck it out!
Matthew 5:27-30

Ezekiel 16:49

Father give a serpent

Alicia alluded to this verse:
Matthew 7:7-11

Strait is the gate
Matthew 7:13-15

Cousin of Danica
Shauna Cee

Subtle attack
offense

Lesson 11
Pornography

Mikayla

#book talk

Smut

Pornography is what we call media that is sexually explicit and designed to appeal to lust in the person viewing it. The Greek word from which the first part of "pornography" comes <porneia> is used dozens of times in the New Testament for fornication or sexual immorality; for instance, Galatians 5:19 calls it one of the works of the flesh. A related word is used for those who practice sexual immorality.

We have studied 1 Peter 4:3 in the *previous lesson* on sensuality. The first sin in the list in that verse could refer to men and women doing things to make others lust, including the use of sexually provocative words and movements (common in dancing). Intentionally watching the things that are done to cause others to lust leaves you no better than those doing them.

Pornography has been around for a very long time; the sin has not changed, but the ease of finding it has dramatically increased in recent years:

▶ In the last generation the Internet has been used to distribute it anonymously (or at least the users think that their use of it cannot be traced) and freely (though it has costs both material and spiritual).

▶ The online security company Webroot says that 2.5 billion emails containing pornography are sent or received each day, 35% of Internet downloads are pornographic, and 34% of Internet users have been exposed to unwanted pornography through ads or misdirected links or emails. Also, 68% of divorce cases involve one of the spouses meeting someone online.[7]

▶ A book by two computational neuroscientists estimated that 4% of the top million websites and 13% of web searches were pornographic.[8] That study (and one of the sites that summarized it) was not likely to have overemphasized the prevalence of pornography.

▶ Much of what could have been considered borderline pornographic a generation ago is now easily available in movies and network television. (Even advertisements on legitimate websites sometimes have suggestive content.) It might not be called pornography; it might be called by a euphemistic name and treated as if it were ordinary, harmless entertainment, but the evil remains the same. Lots of "respectable" entertainment draws viewers and keeps them by making them want to watch people doing sinful things or look at the actors and actresses when they are mostly undressed.

▶ Not only professionally-produced entertainment but also short video clips that many students share among themselves through various apps can be sinful and dangerous to watch.

We are concerned here not only with what society considers pornographic, but with any form of entertainment that appeals to desires that the Bible defines as sinful.

Some People Fail To See the Damage It Causes

I have recently had a student in high school tell me that she saw nothing wrong with working at clubs that specialize in appealing to men's lusts (my words, not hers). Her opinion was that it was just a way to make money. It is hard to believe that she would have thought that most people in those situations were happy and free from abuse, but many people choose to be ignorant of reality. We will see that the Bible makes clear that anything related to pornography and other illicit forms of entertainment is wrong.

Even one of the affected families in a criminal pornography case about which I read years ago said that they were embarrassed that their family member had gotten involved in it, but then they called it a victimless crime. It is foolish to assume that pornography has no victims. It is also foolish to assume that any sin is harmless, but many people do.

· List as many people as you can think of who could be hurt by another person's use of pornography.

The Dangers of Pornography

Pornography is addictive, like many other of Satan's temptations, although calling it an addiction might be abused by some people determined to make every problem an unavoidable sickness for which the "victim" bears no responsibility (see the *third lesson*). This sin is driven by lust, which not only corrupts a person but also sticks a barbed hook in him to pull him further in.

· Several of the actions and desires in **Mark 7:20-23** are related to pornography. According to this passage, what is the source of those things (and thus the source of the choice to view pornography)?

evil within, that defiles a person

Warnings against Pornography and Related Temptations

The Bible tells us how people will try to get others involved in their sexual immorality and what will happen to those who participate in it. Those instructions are also useful in fighting the temptation to watch pornography.

- What will God do to people who participate in sexual immorality (**Hebrews 13:4**)?

  but whoremongers and adulterers God will judge.

- What are the results of following sinful lusts instead of God's word according to **Proverbs 7:24-27**?

  her house is the way to hell, going down to the chambers of death

The Effects of Pornography

Pornography causes its viewers to look upon others as objects to be used rather than as people to be treated with kindness and love. Pornography encourages people to exploit others. The attitudes and actions that come from pornography definitely cause problems in marriages. Pornography distorts the gift of intimacy that God wants a married couple to share and robs that relationship of joy. Pornography also warps the perception of our own bodies that God wants us to have.

- What does **Matthew 5:27-28** say about looking at a woman to lust for her?

  in the heart it was committed

- What does **Matthew 5:29-30** say is better than letting our eyes lead us into sin and being lost? Are we required to take that literally?

  Pluck it out!

- What does **James 1:14-15** say is the end result of allowing our desires to draw us away from the truth?

  lust when concieved brings forth sin sin when finished bringeth death

- What will happen to the lusts of the world (**1 John 2:16-17**)?

  and the world passeth away and lust thereof

The Way To Fight Pornography

Pornography is to be put to death and repudiated. The Bible repeatedly warns us of its dangers (Proverbs 6:23-25). We need to guard our hearts and our eyes by keeping our attention away from the wrong places.

- Colossians 3:5 tells us to put evil desires and passions to death in our lives. What does **Colossians 3:8-10** tell us to do to overcome those temptations and serve Christ faithfully?

  Put on new man, which is renewed in

- How many of the things listed in **Ephesians 5:3-4** could be connected to pornography?

  fornication, uncleaness, filthiness

- Why do we need to work at watching our hearts (**Proverbs 4:23**)?

  Keep thy heart. with all diligence; for out of it are the issues of life

We need to guard our hearts if we want to avoid falling prey to these temptations and if we want to be right with God. Pornography is widely available and we must protect ourselves against it.

Romans 1st COR.

Romans 2:14

without law there is no sin

— Something always have been wrong even before law of Moses, Moral law

we may not fully understand in all ways how God works

I knew a high school student who decided that instead of being "Emily" (not her real name) she wanted to be "Eddie." Eventually she went back to "Emily." I knew several other girls who shaved part of their heads and started holding hands in the halls with other girls. Even in a small town, gender norms are defied – sometimes it even seems like the trendy thing to do.

It was not long ago that our society thoroughly disapproved of same-sex marriage. In 2008, even a liberal presidential candidate would only endorse civil unions and not same-sex marriage. Only seven years later, in 2015 the Supreme Court case *Obergefell v. Hodges* effectively caused same-sex marriage to be guaranteed as a right in every state. The acceptance and promotion of homosexual people in workplaces and public life did not precede the legal decisions by a long time.

A few years ago it was almost unthinkable to be having arguments over which restroom a person should use. There was no debate over having only "Male" and "Female" as options on a form. Now we have people trying to argue that gender is something a person decides and that there could be many different genders. LGBT has become LGBTQ, which may be starting to become LGBTQIA+ or something even longer.

These things are actively promoted in many schools as well. Anti-bullying programs have often had the intent not only to protect children who are different in various ways (the Bible also teaches that no person should be bullied or attacked), but also the intent to promote the acceptance of homosexuality in the schools. Sometimes the anti-bullying programs even try to intimidate those who disagree with their pro-homosexuality stance into silence. Some school employees are afraid to regulate offensive or distracting behavior (if they even recognize it as such) because they are afraid of getting sued or fired.

transgression

Some people demand that others not only use the names they have chosen for themselves but also refer to them not with the regular pronouns "he" or "she," but with "xe" or "ze" or "they" (used as a singular instead of a plural).

Where there is no law ACT there is no transgression

It is not only toleration that is demanded, and not only acceptance, but also approval (see the *sixth lesson*). Lawsuits have been filed against people who will not provide services for same-sex weddings even though the people being sued have done no harm to anyone. Christians today may find themselves similarly targeted.

[handwritten: Jesus justified in turning in Jesus temple — If a gentile in Moses time lied outside of the law would he be saved.]

Homosexuality

While society will often promote the agendas of those who endorse these kinds of sexual immorality and try to persecute those who disagree, God's word is clear in its teaching, whether people want to acknowledge it or not.

- **1 Corinthians 6:9-11** clearly teaches that homosexuality is wrong using two or three different terms; what else does the passage teach that contradicts the statement that people are "born that way" and cannot change their orientation?

  [handwritten: vs. 11 "and such were some of you"]

- What do **Leviticus 18:22** and **20:13** call homosexual behavior?

  [handwritten: Thou shalt not lie with mankind as with womankind: abomination ; death as sentence]

- In **1 Timothy 1:9-11**, the first half of the passage catalogs a number of sins. What does the second half of the passage (the end of Verse 10 and all of Verse 11) say about why those things are wrong?

  [handwritten: Contrary to God's will for Humankind - His creation]

- The uncleanness and dishonoring of the body of **Romans 1:24-25** is connected with which kind of false worship in those verses? *[handwritten: idolatry]*

  [handwritten: -lusts of one's own heart - changed truth of God for a lie; and served creation over creator]

- Which phrase is applied to the practice of homosexuality by both females and males in **Romans 1:26-27**?

  [handwritten: - Vile affection - reprobate : unprincipled; principle- system of belief from chain of reasoning; person]

- The behavior of the men of Sodom in **Genesis 19:4-5** is clearly condemned. How does **Jude 6-7** describe their sins?

  [handwritten: going after strange Flesh]

- Some people read the condemnation of Sodom in **Ezekiel 16:49-50** and say that the real sin of Sodom was not homosexuality, but a lack of

45

hospitality and concern for the poor. While no one should disagree that Sodom lacked hospitality and was not loving, the other part of their claim is not true. How would you respond to the argument about the "real sin?"

Acts 17:19

Denied LORD God & Served self

- In **Judges 19:11-22** we read about behavior toward strangers that was extremely similar to that of the men of Sodom in Genesis 19. Where did that crime take place and why was that ironic?

within *Tribe of* *Benjamin*

Transgender Issues

The practice of dressing as a member of the opposite sex, which has found increasing public acceptance in recent years, is also condemned in the Old Testament. In both testaments the Bible emphasizes the importance of following the gender roles God has created.

love thy neighbor chpt. 22

What does **Deuteronomy 22:5** call the practices of women's wearing men's clothing and men's wearing women's clothing?

read above verse 4 *abomination*

- In **Genesis 1:27** and **5:2**, what phrase is used to describe how God created mankind?

in His own image He created them *- created them and blessed them*

- The words in Genesis about how God created mankind are also quoted with approval by Jesus in **Matthew 19:4**; **Mark 10:6**. Some people claim that Jesus never said anything against homosexuality; what do those verses show about Jesus' teaching on gender roles?

made them male and female *Mark 10:6 addressing evil of divorce*

- What does **1 Corinthians 11:3-6** say that shows that there is a difference in roles for men and women?

- Some people might claim that the difference in roles for men and women in **1 Corinthians 11** is just a reflection of Greek culture two thousand years ago. What does Paul say about the reason for the difference in those roles in **11:7-10** that shows that his teaching applies to all people? *man and woman created for each other*

- Paul also speaks about the difference in men's and women's hair (not in the physical characteristics of the hair itself, but in how it is worn) in **1 Corinthians 11:11-15**. How does **Revelation 9:7-8** show a similar understanding? *"hair of woman" description*

Years ago a syndicated newspaper columnist claimed that the Bible only mentioned homosexuality nine times, so God must not have thought that condemning it was very important. If my Father is telling me something nine times, I hope I am listening to Him! (As you have seen above, there are more than nine relevant passages anyway.) Be willing to stand for the truth even when those around you are actively promoting falsehood.

(End
- Elisabeth's husband
head
- praise God healthy
baby

Lesson 13
"Approv[ing] of Those Who Practice Them" (Romans 1:32)

We have recently studied the increasing public acceptance of homosexuality and transgenderism in opposition to the plain teaching of God's word. Christians, particularly young Christians, may come under a great deal of pressure to go along with what society thinks instead of standing for God's truth. The pressure may be from friends (even some within the church have beliefs about the subject that do not match the Bible); the pressure might also be from schools or workplaces that expect everyone to fall in line behind the leaders and publicly support what the leaders believe is right. I know a few Christians who have left otherwise good jobs because staying in those positions would have required what was essentially a pledge to support pro-homosexual agendas.

We studied Romans 1:24-27 in the *previous lesson*; at the end of that section that describes the state of those who had rejected the knowledge of God and been given over to a debased mind, we read:

> **Romans 1:32** who, knowing the righteous judgment of God, that
> those who practice such things are deserving of death, not only
> do the same but also approve of those who practice them.

It is not only in committing the sins described but also in approving of the people committing them that we can face grave spiritual danger.

We Must Live by God's Standards, Not the World's

Before we look at approving things that are wrong, we will look at the standards by which we determine right and wrong. We need to let God's word show us its standards.

- What must we do to prove the will of God instead of letting our minds be shaped by the world (**Romans 12:1-2**)?

  renewing of mind

- What will happen to everything that the world around us holds dear (**2 Peter 3:10**)?
  - all burned up
  - melt w/ fervent heat

48

- Because we know what will happen to the world, how ought we to live (**2 Peter 3:11-12**)?

  holy conversation & godliness

- What are we warned against doing with unbelievers and why (**2 Corinthians 6:14-17**)?

  unequally yoked with unbelievers
  - be ye separate

- What would be some examples of what 2 Corinthians 6:14 warns us not to do with unbelievers?

  - marry a nonbeliever
  - date someone who is anti-Jesus
  - be best friends with a non-believer

What It Means To Approve of Sin

We have a number of examples in the Bible of people who had not committed certain sins themselves, but approved of those who had. They were still causing problems among God's people. Note that the previous section concerned avoiding the sins approved by the world, but this section emphasizes avoiding the approval of sins committed by unfaithful people who claim to be following God.

- In **Luke 11:47-51**, Jesus pronounces one of the woes against the lawyers. Their fathers had killed the prophets. What were those lawyers doing that showed their approval of their fathers' sin (Verses 47-48)?

  "allow the deeds"
  - built the tombs the murdered prophets are buried in

- As Jesus continued in speaking to the lawyers, what did He show that the lawyers were doing that their fathers had also done (11:49-51)?

  Slay + persecute prophets

- In Acts 7:58, the people from the Council who were stoning Stephen laid their outer clothing at Saul's feet. What did Paul (formerly called Saul) say that his standing by and guarding their clothes had meant (**Acts 8:1**; **22:20**)?

  Consent

- What had been happening in Corinth that had allowed evil people to be approved and recognized by members of the church (**1 Corinthians 11:17-19**)?

49

- In **Romans 14:22,** what did Paul show could happen to a person who personally approved doing something that was actually sinful? (In **14:23,** we see that the same thing could happen to a person who personally doubted that what he was doing was right.)

- What should a Christian do rather than have fellowship with things that are evil (**Ephesians 5:11-13**)?

- What did Paul warn Timothy against doing too quickly that could have led to his sharing in the sin of another person (**1 Timothy 5:21-22**)?

- Why should a Christian neither keep someone in his house who does not teach the truth of the gospel nor greet him (**2 John 10-11**)?

- In **Ezekiel 9,** the LORD was bringing judgment upon Judah for its sin. To avoid punishment, it was not enough just to have not personally committed those sins. What attitude was necessary to be approved by the LORD and spared (**9:4**)?

We Live for God, Not the World

Our purpose on earth is not to be like the world around us.
- For whom must we live (**2 Corinthians 5:15**)?

For whom do you live? Are your choices consistent with what you say that you believe? In this series of lessons the goal has been to strengthen you for the challenges you will face and help you live for God instead of being dragged down to destruction by Satan with the world.

Three bonus lessons follow this one. Please consider them carefully.

Lesson 14
The Abuse of Illegal and Legal Drugs

Drug abuse has long been a problem in our society, especially among young people. Some drugs are legal (for people over certain ages) but dangerous, such as alcohol and nicotine (in tobacco). Some drugs are illegal for practically everyone, such as heroin and fentanyl. Other drugs can be prescribed but are illegal otherwise, such as opioids (pain pills) and methamphetamine. Still others have a confused status; marijuana is still in the most serious category of controlled substance at the federal level in the United States but has been legalized for medical and even "recreational" use in some states.

Some distributors of other drugs try to exploit loopholes or gray areas to get their products to market. A few years ago, packets of dangerous drugs marketed as "bath salts" were sold in many gas stations and convenience stores. They were labeled, "Not for Human Consumption," but they were completely intended to be taken by humans as drugs.

Many controversial claims are made about various drugs. Some people say that marijuana is harmless or even beneficial. Others may concede that marijuana has dangers, but is at least safer than tobacco products, alcohol, or narcotics. Vaping products have been marketed as safer than cigarettes and helpful for people who want to quit smoking. As of this writing, more studies and reports have been published that make the claims of harmlessness much harder to believe.

Some people think that legalizing drugs will remove many of the problems associated with drug abuse, such as violence among dealers and users and impurities in the drugs (not that they are not dangerous in their pure form). However, prescription drugs like opioids are highly regulated but still cause problems when abused. Even some legal stimulants (such as caffeine, particularly in the large amounts found in energy drinks) can be taken in dangerous quantities. Even if man makes something legal, its use may not fit God's will for us.

Many people have an attitude that makes them more likely to abuse drugs. It is connected to sensuality (the *tenth lesson*): having a certain feeling can become more important than being healthy and righteous to them. They often choose not to be satisfied in life without turning to some sort of chemical. They are looking for happiness but not looking to their Creator. The attitude that something in a pill, powder, vapor, can, or syringe will bring more meaning to life is a source of the problem with drugs. When that attitude is combined with the rejection of personal responsibility (the *third lesson*), the problem gets worse.

Biblical Examples of the Use and Abuse of Drugs

I have known a couple of Christians who wanted me to approve of the use of alcohol (the Bible does not always totally condemn it but I do not endorse its use); each of those people apparently later indulged in alcohol or another drug. Christians need to be aware of the dangers and stay away!

- According to Paul in **1 Timothy 5:23**, under what circumstances could Timothy's consuming wine have been beneficial?

- List the phrases that show the deceptive nature of alcohol in **Proverbs 23:29-35**. These descriptions would often also apply to other drugs.

- Why were kings and princes warned against drinking wine in **Proverbs 31:4-5**? Would those reasons have application to other people?

 · How many of the things mentioned in **1 Peter 4:3** were associated with the abuse of alcohol?

Drug abuse is not new, although man has discovered new ways to abuse pharmaceuticals as his knowledge of chemistry has grown.

- **Galatians 5:19-21** lists the works of the flesh. The second term in 5:20 is "sorcery" or "witchcraft" in most translations; in Greek the word is *pharmakeia*. Which English word has come from that Greek word? What could that indicate about what people two thousand years ago used in practicing sorcery?

Five Important Biblical Questions about the Use of Drugs

Many dubious claims are made about various drugs by those who encourage their use. How can we cut through the confusion to determine what is acceptable to God? What are the questions we should ask about using any drug?

1. Is it illegal?
· How many of the laws of our society are we supposed to obey "for the Lord's sake" (**1 Peter 2:13-14**)?

· Whom would we ultimately be disobeying by refusing to obey our government's laws about drugs (**Romans 13:1-2**)?

2. Is it intoxicating (causing an altered state in the brain)?
· What kind of behavior is commanded for older men in **Titus 2:2** that is also commanded for younger men in **Titus 2:6** and all Christians in **Titus 2:12**?

· Why are Christians told to sober and vigilant (both of these qualities are negatively affected by drug abuse) in **1 Peter 5:8**?

3. Is it addictive or habit-forming (causing dependence)?
· Which phrase in **1 Corinthians 6:12** showed Paul's attitude about keeping control of himself?

4. Is it unsafe (not whether it is relatively less dangerous than something else)?
Even _if_ marijuana is relatively more safe than tobacco and even _if_ vaping is relatively more safe than smoking, that does not make either using marijuana or vaping good. Is jumping off 25-foot cliffs safer than jumping off 50-foot cliffs? I suppose, but why would we think that God approved of jumping off either for no good reason?
· Please read **Colossians 3:16-17**. Whom should each of our words and actions honor? Does having our minds affected by drug abuse help us honor Him?

5. Does it have a bad influence upon others?

· Look at the ways in which Timothy was told to be a good example to other Christians in **1 Timothy 4:12**. In which of those areas would drug abuse harm our ability to be good examples?

example of believers in word and conversation, conduct

· Think about the influence that one person's abuse of drugs has upon younger people. What did Jesus say would be better than causing a young person who believes in Him to sin in **Matthew 18:5-6**?

In the next few years, the problem of drug abuse is very likely to continue. While the specific drugs and methods of consumption will likely change, the principles of God's word will not. Christians need to find their purpose in satisfaction in serving God and serving others and Christians must learn to handle the problems of life in a Biblical way.

Lesson 15
Calling-Out Culture: Shaming All Who Disagree

Some people in our society apply the label "racist" to anyone who disagrees with them about illegal immigration. Someone who does not want people to enter the country illegally might be called racist despite having no hatred of any race or nationality.

Similarly, a person who does not agree that homosexual behavior should be approved (the *twelfth lesson*) might be called "homophobic." Why? The suffix -phobic means that you are afraid of something, but many label those (especially Christians) who speak against homosexuality as homophobic without any evidence of fear.

We live in a culture in which many people attribute evil motives to anyone who disagrees with them. Many people show that they attribute evil motives to others when they publicly call out and shame those with whom they disagree. Those people who justify trying to silence others who disagree with them and justify trying to destroy their influence with others are exalting themselves.

False and True Enlightenment

Many people like to think of themselves as enlightened or knowledgeable about what is important. A term that gained popularity in the late 2010s, especially among those with a secular worldview (see the *first lesson*), is "woke." Being woke seems to combine thinking that your judgments are unquestionably right with thinking that your motivations are unquestionably pure. Unfortunately, people who feel that way usually do not base their beliefs upon the real source of enlightenment and knowledge, which is God's word.

The Bible often describes those who know the truth as "enlightened." The issue is not whether someone can be enlightened or "woke", but which beliefs make a person truly enlightened and spiritually awake.

· What does the Psalmist say is the true source of enlightenment in **Psalm 18:27-28**?

the LORD My God

· **Psalm 19:7-11** says that God's commandments enlighten the eyes.

the Law of the LORD

Which other phrases in that passage describe the effect that the words or laws of God have upon someone who loves them?

- What allows us to have the eyes of our understanding enlightened in **Ephesians 1:17-18**?

    Spirit of understanding and wisdom

The Biblical Sense of Being Awake and Aware

We need to be aware of the spiritual reality around us. The Bible tells us to be aware or spiritually awake, but that awareness does not come from human knowledge.

- People often wake up when the light hits them. What is described as darkness in **Ephesians 5:11-14**? What is the source of the light?

- Why does Paul tell his Roman readers to wake up in a spiritual sense (**Romans 13:11-12**)?

- Paul also tells his readers to walk the right way, as in daytime, in **Romans 13:13-14**. What kinds of sins were the opposite of walking in that way?

- Please read **1 Corinthians 15:33-34**. What are some ways in which even Christians could fail to be awake to righteousness?

False and True Shame

Many people in our society react negatively to attempts to help and correct others. Trying to help an obese person regarding nutrition and exercise can be called "body-shaming." Many people want to be "body-positive," telling others that their bodies are great as they are and implying that they do not need to change, even if their current choices are causing themselves harm. People who encourage others to change for the better in matters of sin (repentance) can also be accused of "shaming." Ironically, a culture that often thinks of constructive criticism as "shaming" sometimes employs destructive public shaming to try to enforce its will.

There is a real sense of shame that people should feel when they have done something wrong. God's word shows the difference between that and the false sense of shame that the world sometimes uses.

- What or whom has God put to shame with things that some considered weak and foolish (**1 Corinthians 1:26-29**)?

- What was the sinful and destructive practice among the Corinthian Christians that Paul said was shameful (**1 Corinthians 6:1-5**)?

- How could the abuse of the Lord's Supper in Corinth have caused the poor Christians there to suffer undeserved shame (**1 Corinthians 11:20-22**)?

- With whom did Paul tell Christians not to eat in order to cause that person a necessary sense of shame (**2 Thessalonians 3:14**)?

- Of which two things did Paul tell Timothy not to be ashamed in **2 Timothy 1:8**?

- What kind of undeserved shame do you think Jesus suffered on the cross (**Hebrews 12:2-3**)?

Sinful Pride about Opinions and Judgments

Someone who is willing to hurt or humiliate someone for disagreeing with his or her opinions often has a problem with pride. Some of those who have rejected God's revealed truth treat their own judgments as infallible. Christians can fall into a similar trap. One of the false teachings that damaged the church in its first two centuries was called Gnosticism, based on the Greek word *gnosis*, "knowledge." Some believed that they could gain a personal knowledge of God that was better than the Bible's teaching. Few today would try to teach that, but it is not hard to become attached to our own opinions and judgments to the extent that we become sinfully proud of them and look down upon others.

- What does too much trust in one's own knowledge do to a person (**1 Corinthians 8:1**)? What is the true state of that person's knowledge (**1 Corinthians 8:2**)?

- What had happened to Christians who had followed a false knowledge (**1 Timothy 6:20-21**)?

The Need for Consistency and Humility

All people deserve to be treated kindly as long as they are not seeking to harm others, and Christians are commanded to love even their enemies (Matthew 5:43-45; Luke 6:27-36). We can fight the temptation to mistreat those who disagree by seeking to live consistently with our profession of faith and by being humble.

- How should a servant of the Lord act toward those who oppose the truth (**2 Timothy 2:24-26**)?

- What did some people say to others that made God very angry in **Isaiah 65:2-5**? What word to we use to describe people who say one thing while acting in the opposite way?

Conflict in society provides the temptation to mistreat those who disagree with us while congratulating ourselves for our wisdom. A proper respect for God's word will give us a true understanding of spiritual reality while remaining humble, as He wills us to be.

Lesson 16

Broken Families

[handwritten: 40-50% marriage end in divorce → women have discontent]

We live in a society with many broken families. In my work as a substitute teacher, I do not make the assumption that children have a mother and a father at home. In some of my classes in a small-town school that serves a rural area, a large majority of students do not live with both of their biological parents. One high school student told me recently that she did not have any friends who lived with both parents.

Why We Have This Problem

Over the past few decades, the number of children born to parents who are not married to each other has grown dramatically. Fifty years ago, approximately one out of every ten children in the United States was born that way. Now it is four out of ten. In those fifty years, the population of the United States has almost doubled, but the number of divorced people is about six times larger than it was. Though the percentage of people who are divorced has stabilized in the last twenty years, the percentage of people who are married has decreased significantly and the percentage of

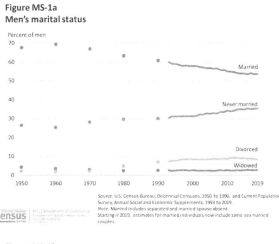

Figure MS-1a
Men's marital status

Source: U.S. Census Bureau, Decennial Censuses, 1950 to 1990, and Current Population Survey, Annual Social and Economic Supplements, 1993 to 2019.
Note: Married includes separated and married spouse absent.
Starting in 2019, estimates for married individuals now include same-sex married couples.

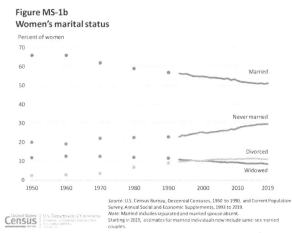

Figure MS-1b
Women's marital status

Source: U.S. Census Bureau, Decennial Censuses, 1950 to 1990, and Current Population Survey, Annual Social and Economic Supplements, 1993 to 2019.
Note: Married includes separated and married spouse absent.
Starting in 2019, estimates for married individuals now include same-sex married couples.

U.S. Census Historical Data on Marital Status[9]

people who have never married has increased significantly. Many more people are now living together without marriage. Those unmarried relationships are much less stable than married relationships. These changes have caused more children to be raised without attachment to two married parents.

What God's Word Says

Though society has changed, God's will has not changed. God wants marriages to stay together.

- What did Jesus say was the only acceptable reason for divorce in **Matthew 5:31-32**?

  sexual immorality

God does not want divorce to happen generally, though divorce is permitted in the circumstance mentioned above.

- What does God say about divorce in **Malachi 2:16**?

Many families in our society are broken, and even when new families are formed from these broken families, they may be in violation of Christ's teaching (Luke 16:18; 1 Corinthians 7:10-11).

- How did Jesus describe the sin committed by a person who divorces his or her spouse for an unscriptural reason and then remarries (**Mark 10:11-12**)?

The Effect upon Our Families

It has always been risky to marry someone who is not a Christian, but it probably has become more so and may become more dangerous still. A few generations ago, if you were to marry someone who was not a Christian but generally had good morals and an appreciation for the family, perhaps you could be fairly confident that you would stay married. Making that assumption when most of society does not see fornication (sexual activity outside of marriage) as a problem is dangerous.

The effects of broken families tend to continue through at least the next generation. The lack of a loving, unified home hurts young people; despite that hurt, they often repeat the hurtful behaviors they have seen in their parents.

The Bible frequently mentions those who do not have fathers as special objects of concern (Deuteronomy 24:17-21). In our society, abuse, abandonment, divorce, and imprisonment leave many children effectively fatherless even if their fathers are still alive. Some of the young children I teach in the schools seem to have no idea how to react to a male authority figure because they have no father in their lives. The lack of guidance from a father will also hurt them later in life.

This lesson is not teaching that family is required for faithfulness. The Ethiopian (Acts 8:26-40) may have had no family at all. Many who are deprived of a physical family are still blessed (Psalm 113:9).

· What does **Psalm 68:5-6** portray God as doing for people who are solitary or lonely?

The Lord wants to help all people and gladly accepts those who obey Him no matter what kind of family background they might have had growing up.

Following God's plan for the development of the family helps everyone, but His principles for the family are receiving increasingly less attention in our society.

The Effect upon the Church

When the world experiences widespread problems with a particular kind of sin (for examples, see *most of our previous lessons*), those problems usually cause issues within the church. A great danger to church unity in the last few decades has been false teaching on divorce and remarriage. Many individual Christians have the burden of divorce within their lives, often through no fault of their own.

Christians who seek to follow the command to teach others the gospel (2 Timothy 2:2) will likely find more of the people in the world facing additional obstacles to conversion. Someone who is living with another person while unmarried will face great difficulty in changing that living situation to match God's word. Someone who has remarried in a way the New Testament does not allow will face great difficulty in fully obeying Christ's teaching.

The Old Testament illustrates some of the problems that came to the Israelites when they had ignored the rules about marriage that God had given them.

· What had God told the people of Israel not to do regarding marriage in **Ezra 9:10-12**?

Christians and their children who are part of broken families will usually find less consistent instruction in God's word and less stability in their home lives than other Christian families would.

The Way To Fight Its Effects

Even when society has failed to follow God's will for the family, Christians can still follow God's principles and work at building families that honor Him. What are the steps that people who have young families or have not yet started their own families should take?

· In **Deuteronomy 6:6-9**, what did God tell the Israelites to do to keep His words in the hearts of their children and families?

· List two things that the worthy woman does in **Proverbs 31:26-27** to help her family grow to honor the Lord.

· In **Ephesians 6:4**, what are fathers to avoid as they train their children to obey the Lord?

· Older women are to teach younger women to love their husbands and children in **Titus 2:3-5**. Most people have affection for children and spouses without being taught. What are some ways (that do not come so easily) in which people should be taught to love their family members?

Families are the building blocks of society. When the building blocks break, the entire structure is in danger. Congregations are also hurt by family problems. Following God's will in this area will help us obey Him in many other ways.

Endnotes

1   For an example of a psychological group who differed, see https://en.wikipedia.org/wiki/DSM-5#British_Psychological_Society_response, retrieved on 9 October 2019: The British Psychological Society criticized the DSM-5 as having designated diseases in a way that was "clearly based largely on social norms, with 'symptoms' that all rely on subjective judgements… not value-free, but rather reflect[ing] current normative social expectations".

2   https://www.nytimes.com/2018/10/15/obituaries/herbert-d-kleber-dead.html, Katharine Q. Seelye, "Herbert D. Kleber, Pioneer in Addiction Treatment, Dies at 84", *The New York Times*, 15 October 2018, retrieved on 1 October 2019.

3   Jean Twenge, "Why it matters that teens are reading less", *The Conversation* website, 20 August 2018, http://theconversation.com/why-it-matters-that-teens-are-reading-less-99281, retrieved on 8 November 2019.

4   "Block explicit lyrics in music subscription services", https://www.cnet.com/how-to/block-explicit-lyrics-in-music-subscription-services/, retrieved on 18 September 2019.

5   https://www.billboard.com/charts/year-end/2018/hot-100-songs for songs (retrieved on 19 November 2019 and 25 October 2020) and metrolyrics.com for content under specific song names (retrieved on 20 November 2019 and 25 October 2020). Google Translate was used to make counts of Bad Bunny's and J Balvin's Spanish lyrics.

6   https://www.the-numbers.com/box-office-records/domestic/all-movies/cumulative/released-in-2018 and https://www.the-numbers.com/box-office-records/domestic/all-movies/cumulative/released-in-2019 for the movies and https://www.kids-in-mind.com under the name of each movie on the list for the counts of objectionable material, retrieved on 19 November 2019 and updated on 27 December 2019. Please note that movies that were released late in 2019 (e.g., *Frozen II* and *Star Wars: The Rise of Skywalker*) had much higher gross revenues once 2020 sales had been added to the total.

7   https://www.webroot.com/us/en/resources/tips-articles/internet-pornography-by-the-numbers, retrieved on 4 December 2019.

8   Ogas, Ogi, Ph.D. and Sai Gaddam, Ph.D. A Billion Wicked Thoughts: What the Internet Tells Us About Sex and Relationships. Cited in Michael Castleman's "Dueling Statistics: How Much of the Internet is Porn?" in *Psychology Today* online as a more realistic estimate than those of Internet filtering software companies. https://www.psychologytoday.com/us/blog/all-about-sex/201611/dueling-statistics-how-much-the-internet-is-porn, retrieved on 4 December 2019.

9   These United States Census Bureau charts and more are available at https://www.census.gov/content/dam/Census/library/visualizations/time-series/demo/families-and-households/ms-1a.pdf and https://www.census.gov/content/dam/Census/library/visualizations/time-series/demo/families-and-households/ms-1b.pdf. Retrieved on 16 December 2019.

Words of Thanks

Thank you to those who have studied through the material with me at the Hillcrest Church of Christ or have made suggestions about the book:

Joy and Grace Brailey, Alyssa Gabriel, Shelby Glaub, Clay Prouty, Samuel Schlabach, Christopher Trost, Nathan, Samuel, and Logan Whitney, and Nichole Williams

Special thanks are given to Sharon Brailey for her help with the book in many ways.

teen Alicia - talking to a boy
adult Alicia - talking to parents about spiritual
                matters

Lydia - joke about diseases that they have
            no' idea about
Emma - talking to other people
Capri - talkin
Abbi - speaking in public
Isabel - pulbic pda (homosexuality)
Danica - public reading
Sophia - backbiting
Dani - Silence
Julieta - staring

Helena Reynolds April 19th birthday
Claire Graham   April 24th

Made in the USA
Coppell, TX
13 November 2022

86297876R00037